Presented

in memory of

Katharine

Edmonds

The Fall of the Berlin Wall

written by **Joeming Dunn**
illustrated by **Ben Dunn**

magic
wagon

visit us at
www.abdopublishing.com

Published by Magic Wagon, a division of the ABDO Publishing Group, 8000 West 78th Street, Edina, Minnesota 55439. Copyright © 2009 by Abdo Consulting Group, Inc. International copyrights reserved in all countries. All rights reserved. No part of this book may be reproduced in any form without written permission from the publisher.
Graphic Planet™ is a trademark and logo of MagicWagon.

Printed in the United States.

Written by Joeming Dunn
Illustrated by Ben Dunn
Edited by Stephanie Hedlund and Rochelle Baltzer
Interior layout and design by Antarctic Press
Cover art by Ben Dunn
Cover design by Neil Klinepier

Library of Congress Cataloging-in-Publication Data

Dunn, Joeming W.
  The fall of the Berlin Wall / written by Joeming Dunn ; illustrated by Ben Dunn.
    p. cm. -- (Graphic history)
  ISBN 978-1-60270-182-3
  1. Berlin Wall, Berlin, Germany, 1961-1989--Juvenile literature. 2. Berlin (Germany)--Politics and government--1945-1990--Juvenile literature. 3. Cold War--Juvenile literature. I. Dunn, Ben. II. Title.
DD881.D84 2009
943.087--dc22
                                    2007051628

TABLE of CONTENTS

Timeline

1945 - The Soviet army captured Berlin in May from the Nazis during World War II; the city was divided into east and west sectors.

1947 to 1948 - The Cold War began between the United States and Soviet Union.

1949 - The Federal Republic of Germany, or West Germany, was founded on May 12. On May 24, the German Democratic Republic, or East Germany, was founded.

1952 - All borders except Brandenburg Gate were closed between East and West Germany on May 26.

1961 - On August 13, soldiers began building the Berlin Wall; the Brandenburg Gate between East and West Berlin was closed on August 14.

1963 - U.S. president John F. Kennedy visited the wall.

1987 - U.S. president Ronald Reagan visited Berlin and urged Soviet leader Mikhail Gorbachev to tear down the wall.

1989 - The Hungarian government opened its border with Austria between May and September. Thousands of East Germans made their way to West Germany.

1989 - On November 9, thousands of East German protesters went to border crossings demanding they be let through. The border guards stood back as thousands streamed into West Berlin. The wall was breached and people began to pull it down in celebration.

1990 - East and West Germany were formally reunited on October 3.

EAST PRUSSIA

WEST PRUSSIA

GERMANY

NETHERLANDS

BELGIUM

POLAND

UPPER SILESIA

LUXEMBOURG
ALSACE-LORRAINE

CZECHOSLOVAKIA

FRANCE

SWITZERLAND

AUSTRIA

HUNGARY

Germany 1933

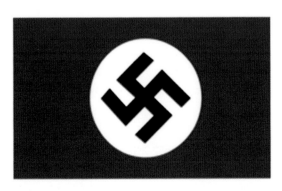

The Saar	
The Ruhr	
German territory	
Sudetenland	
Rhineland (demilitarized zone)	

Germany's Rulers

5

On January 30, 1933, Nazi Party leader Adolf Hitler became chancellor of Germany.

Soon after, Hitler declared war on Poland and began World War II.

Allied countries of the United States, Britain, France, and the Soviet Union joined forces. Their aim was to stop the threat of Nazi Germany.

The combined forces of the Allies blocked Hitler's plan to take over the world.

On May 8, 1945, the German forces announced unconditional surrender. Victory in Europe was declared.

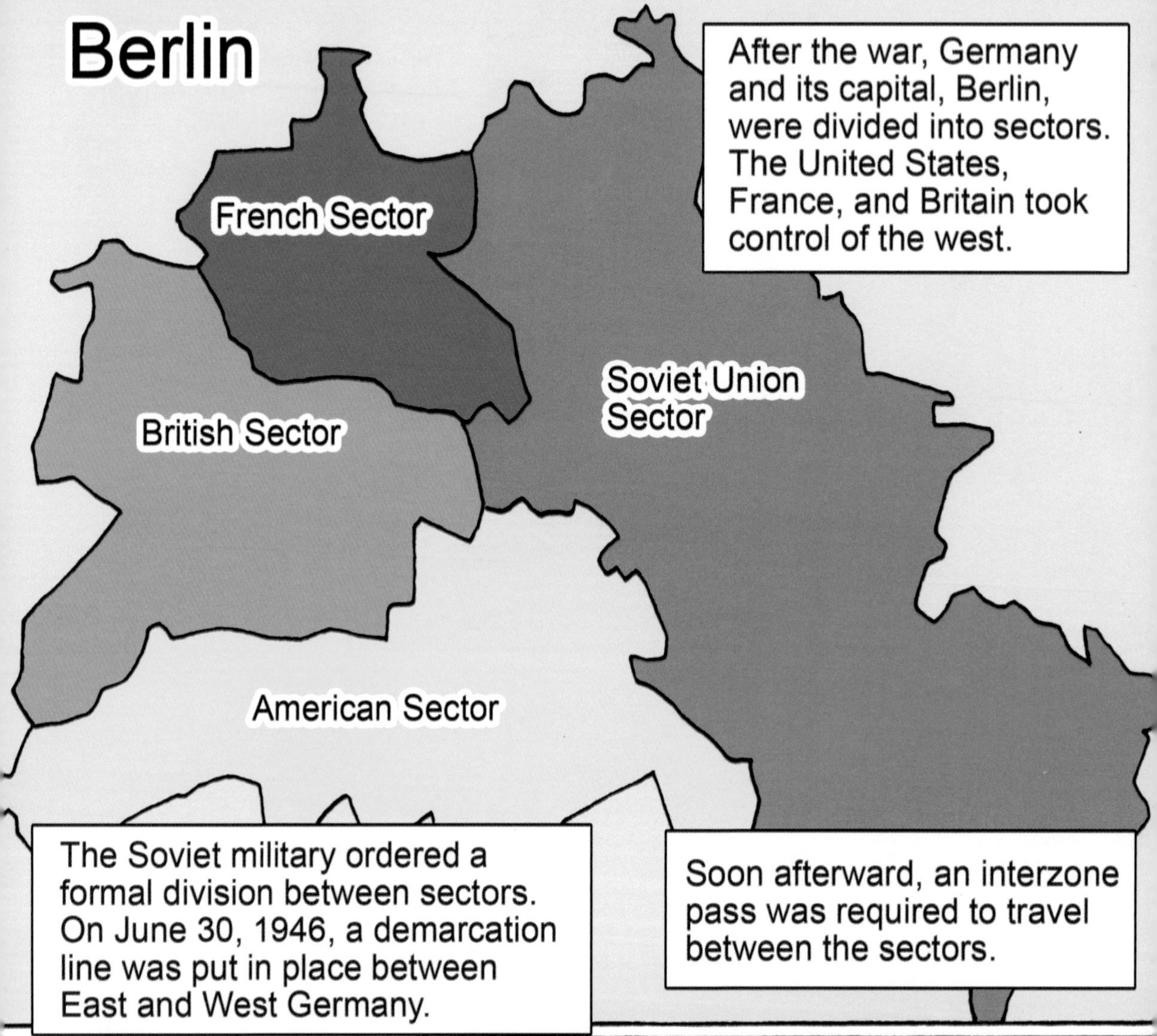
Berlin
After the war, Germany and its capital, Berlin, were divided into sectors. The United States, France, and Britain took control of the west.
French Sector
Soviet Union Sector
British Sector
American Sector
The Soviet military ordered a formal division between sectors. On June 30, 1946, a demarcation line was put in place between East and West Germany.
Soon afterward, an interzone pass was required to travel between the sectors.

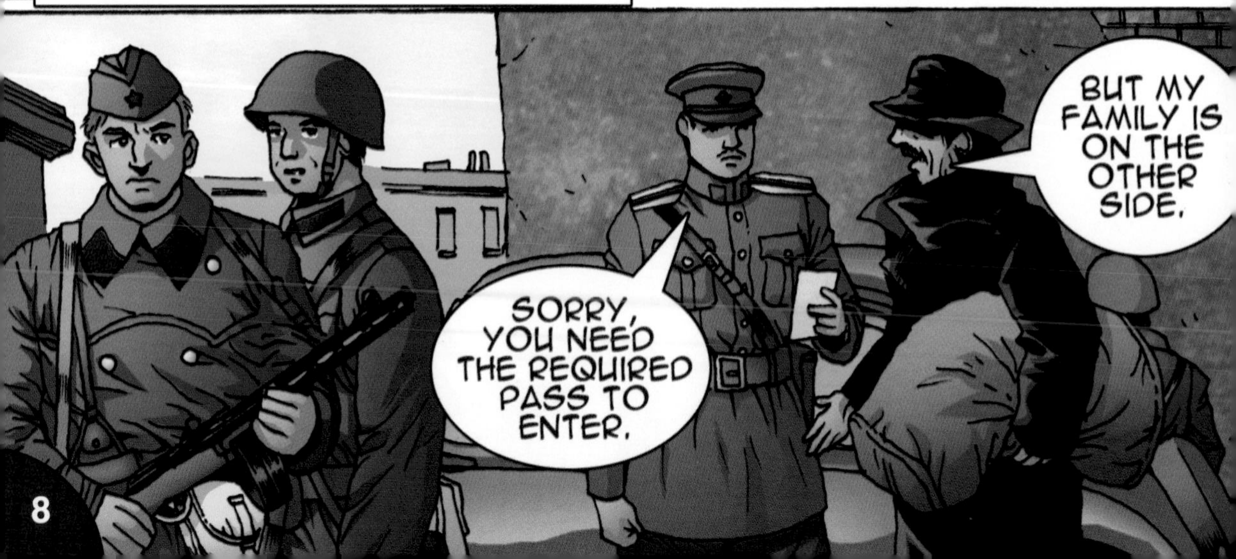
BUT MY FAMILY IS ON THE OTHER SIDE.
SORRY, YOU NEED THE REQUIRED PASS TO ENTER.

The United States, Britain, and France wanted Germany to be independent again. So, they established a new currency and began rebuilding.

The Soviet Union viewed this as trying to take power away from them. This began the Cold War.

During this time, U.S. president Harry S. Truman adopted a new doctrine. It limited the Soviet Union's power. But, the leader of the Soviet Union, Joseph Stalin, wanted more control of eastern Europe.

On June 24, 1948, the Soviet Union responded to the changes. It established a blockade of the western part of Berlin. No food or supplies could enter through eastern Berlin.

The hope was to isolate Berliners so that the Soviet Union could take control.

PA, WHEN CAN WE EAT?

WE HAVE TO CONSERVE OUR FOOD.

WE DON'T KNOW WHEN WE CAN GET MORE.

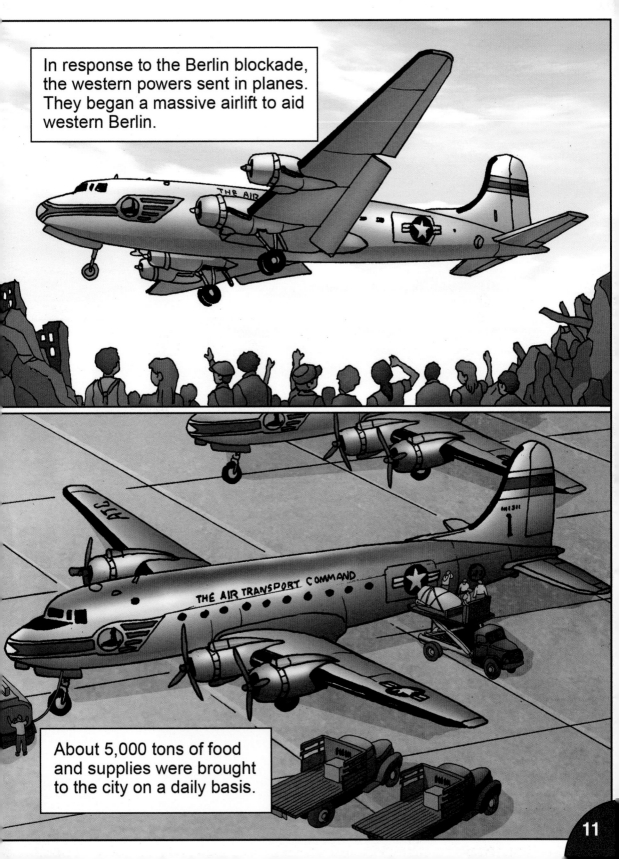

In response to the Berlin blockade, the western powers sent in planes. They began a massive airlift to aid western Berlin.

THE AIR TRANSPORT COMMAND

About 5,000 tons of food and supplies were brought to the city on a daily basis.

Due to the airlift, the blockade ended on May 12, 1949. Shipments to West Germany by road and rail resumed.

Soon after, the Federal Republic of Germany established a new government for West Germans.

Berlin

East Germany

West Germany

In response, the East German government became the German Democratic Republic.

On May 26, 1952, all borders between East and West Germany were closed. The only border opening was between East and West Germany at the Brandenburg Gate.

Chapter 3 East vs. West Germany

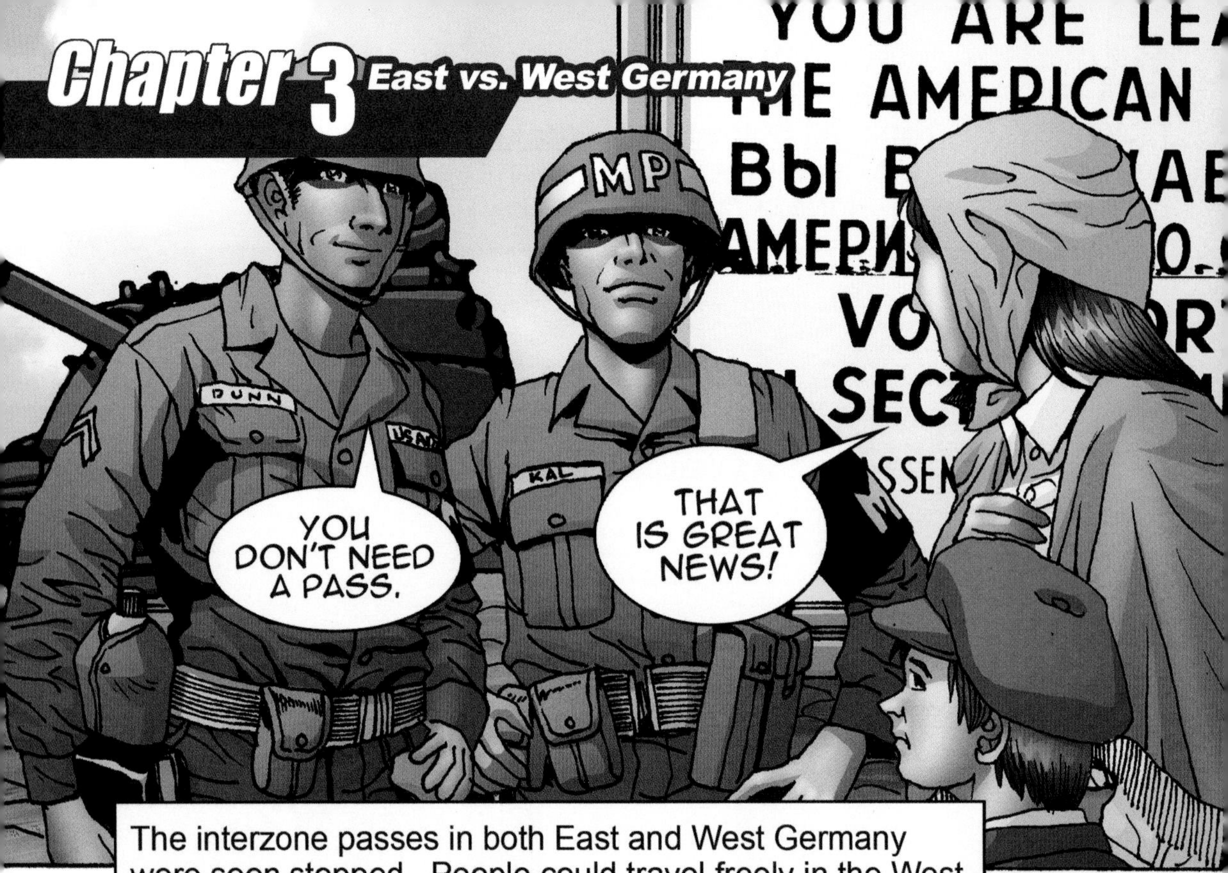
THE AMERICAN
MP
DUNN
KAL
YOU DON'T NEED A PASS.
THAT IS GREAT NEWS!

The interzone passes in both East and West Germany were soon stopped. People could travel freely in the West. But in the East, permission was still required for travel.

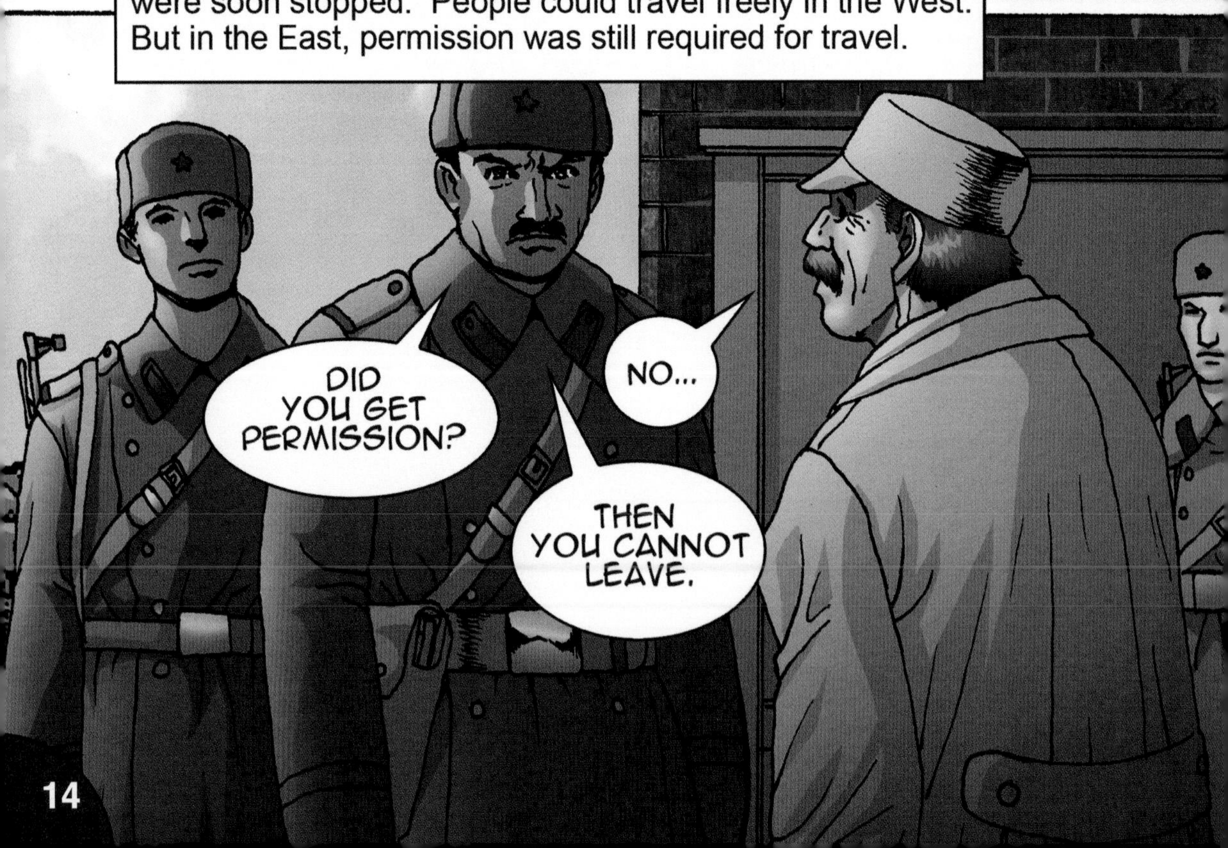
DID YOU GET PERMISSION?
NO...
THEN YOU CANNOT LEAVE.

Travel between East and West Germany became more difficult. On December 11, 1957, a law was established in East Germany.

It allowed a sentence of up to three years in prison for leaving without permission.

During this time, the Cold War grew worse between the Soviet Union and the United States.

In the United States, there was a great deal of suspicion about communism. Julius and Ethel Rosenberg were executed for spying for the Soviet Union.

Vietnamese communists defeated the French, who were controlling North Vietnam. South Vietnam was protected by the United States.

The space race also started in 1957. The Soviet Union began it by launching the first satellite into space. This satellite was called Sputnik.

The communist influence came close to the United States in 1959. That year, communist leader Fidel Castro took control of Cuba.

The United States was concerned about communism. It was prepared to use nuclear attacks on the Soviet Union to defend its people.

In 1960, a spy plane from the United States was shot down over the Soviet Union. This increased the tensions between the countries.

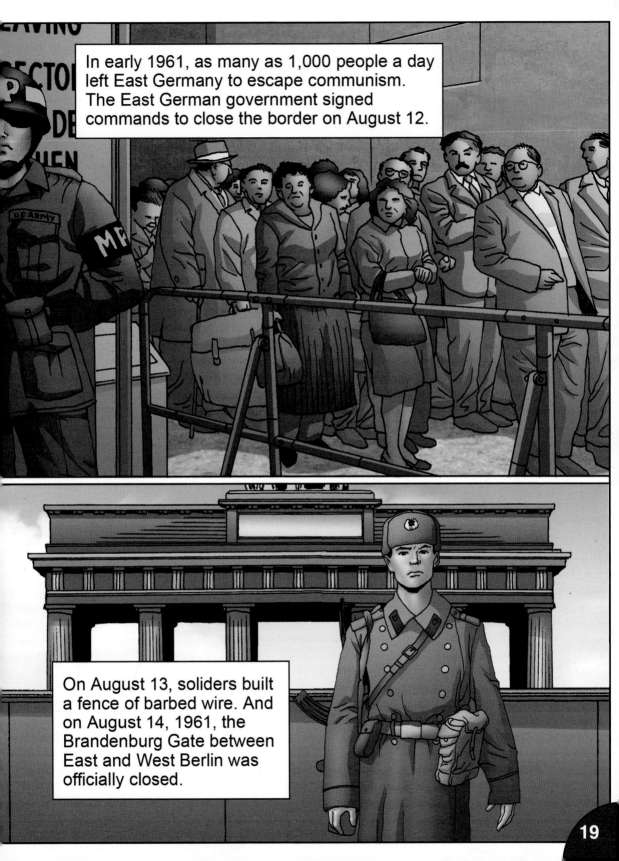

In early 1961, as many as 1,000 people a day left East Germany to escape communism. The East German government signed commands to close the border on August 12.

On August 13, soliders built a fence of barbed wire. And on August 14, 1961, the Brandenburg Gate between East and West Berlin was officially closed.

The only travel point between East and West Germany was now closed. Many families were separated. Even phone lines and mail services were cut between the areas.

A cement wall was then constructed to prevent further migration.

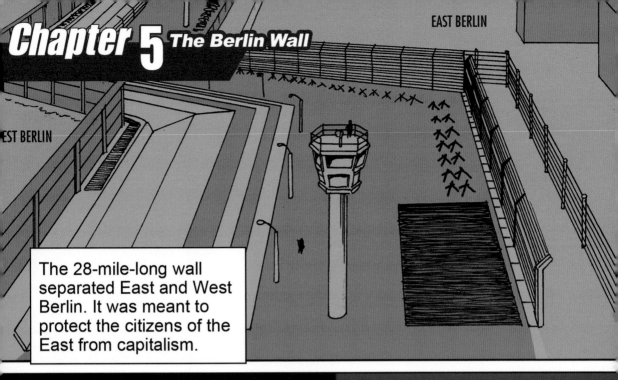

EAST BERLIN

EST BERLIN

The 28-mile-long wall separated East and West Berlin. It was meant to protect the citizens of the East from capitalism.

In response to the wall, U.S. president John F. Kennedy made a visit to Berlin. He proclaimed *Ich bin ein Berliner*, which means "I am a citizen of Berlin."

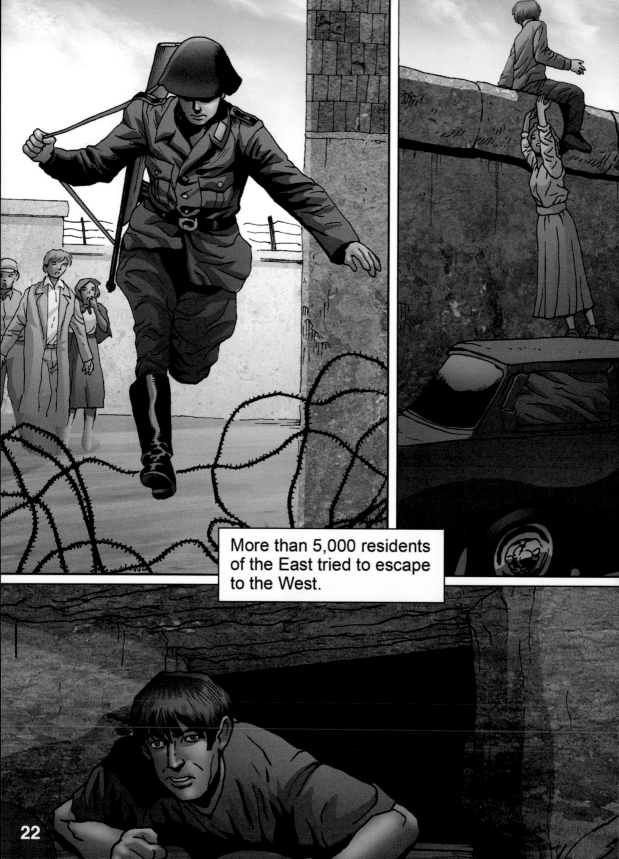

More than 5,000 residents of the East tried to escape to the West.

Many attempts were met with deadly force.

On August 17, 1962, 18-year-old Peter Fechter tried to jump the wall. But he was shot by soldiers. He was one of nearly 200 people to die during their escape attempts.

Despite the news restrictions from the West, East Germans found ways of getting information. Some used journalists to sneak books across the borders.

On September 3, 1971, the United States, Britain, France, and the Soviet Union met. They improved the trade and travel restrictions between East and West Germany. This helped the people, and fewer tried to escape.

In the early 1980s, the relationship between the Soviet Union and the United States began to improve. A treaty was signed that restricted the use of medium and short-range nuclear weapons.

Many former Soviet-controlled countries began to declare independence. One of the first was Poland, which was led by Lech Walesa. Hungary soon followed.

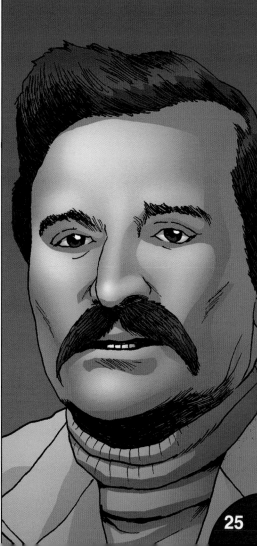

Chapter 6 The Wall Falls

On June 12, 1987, U.S. president Ronald Reagan made a trip to West Berlin. He sent a message to Mikhail Gorbachev, the leader of the Soviet Union.

MR. GORBACHEV, TEAR DOWN THIS WALL.

In his speech to citizens of West Berlin, President Reagan gave an emotional request.

In September 1989, the Hungarian government allowed open travel between Hungary and Austria. Many East Germans took advantage of this. By the end of September, 30,000 East Germans had fled to the West.

East Germany tried to stop travel to Hungary.

Many East Germans begged for asylum in West Germany embassies in Poland and Czechoslovakia.

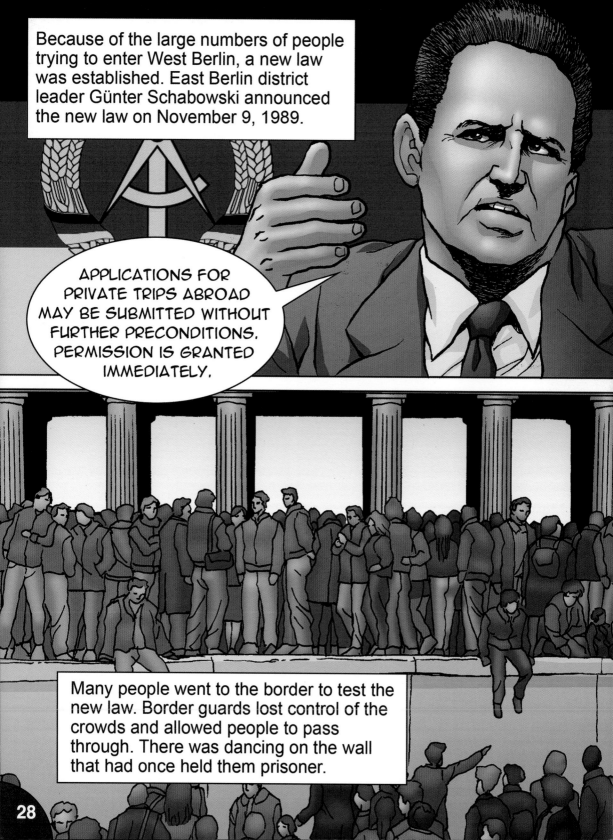

Because of the large numbers of people trying to enter West Berlin, a new law was established. East Berlin district leader Günter Schabowski announced the new law on November 9, 1989.

APPLICATIONS FOR PRIVATE TRIPS ABROAD MAY BE SUBMITTED WITHOUT FURTHER PRECONDITIONS. PERMISSION IS GRANTED IMMEDIATELY.

Many people went to the border to test the new law. Border guards lost control of the crowds and allowed people to pass through. There was dancing on the wall that had once held them prisoner.

The gates were opened, and the Berlin Wall fell on November 9, 1989. All Germans were free. Soon afterward, the Soviet Union was dissolved as well.

Fast Facts

* On August 12, 1961, Walter Ulbricht, the East German leader, signed the commands to close the border between East and West Germany.

* The Berlin Wall started as barbed wire and light fencing. Over the years, it was built into a complex series of three walls. It had fences topped with barbed wire, gun positions, and watchtowers. All were heavily guarded and patrolled.

* By the 1980s, the wall was as tall as 15 feet (5 m) in some places. It extended 28 miles (45 km) through Berlin. It also extended 75 miles (121 km) around West Berlin, separating it from the rest of East Germany.

* About 5,000 East Germans managed to cross the Berlin Wall and reach West Berlin safely. East German authorities captured another 5,000 during their attempt. And, 191 were killed while crossing the wall.

* The Brandenburg Gate was the last passage closed between East and West Germany. It was reopened on December 22, 1989. It remains a symbol of the reunification of Germany.

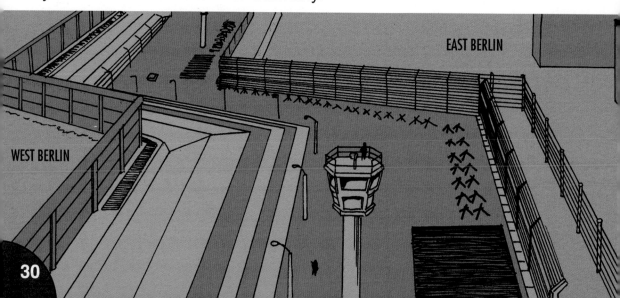

EAST BERLIN

WEST BERLIN

Glossary

allies - people or countries that agree to help each other in times of need.

asylum - an institution that protects and cares for those in need, especially the mentally ill, the poor, or orphans.

blockade - the prevention of supplies or troops from going into or out of an area.

capitalism - an economic system where businesses compete to sell their products and services.

communism - a social and economic system in which everything is owned by the government and given to the people as needed. A person who believes in communism is called a communist.

demarcation line - a boundary that establishes a border between two areas.

embassy - the home and office of a diplomat who lives in a foreign country.

Nazi - a member of the German political party that controlled Germany under Adolf Hitler.

nuclear - of or relating to the energy created when atoms are divided or combined. An atomic bomb is a nuclear weapon.

Web Sites

To learn more about the Berlin Wall, visit ABDO Publishing Company on the World Wide Web at **www.abdopublishing.com**. Web sites about the Berlin Wall are featured on our Book Links page. These links are routinely monitored and updated to provide the most current information available.

Index